the NATURE *of* JOYFUL Relationships

the NATURE *of* JOYFUL Relationships

*Inspiring Tails from the Animal Kingdom
to Transform Your life*

Photo Credit: James Balog/The Image Bank/Getty Images

DENISE DONATO-McCONNELL

NEW YORK

the NATURE *of* JOYFUL Relationships

Inspiring Tails from the Animal Kingdom to Transform Your life

ISBN 978-1-61448-359-5 paperback
ISBN 978-1-61448-360-1 eBook
Library of Congress Control Number: 2012945498

Morgan James Publishing
The Entrepreneurial Publisher
5 Penn Plaza, 23rd Floor
New York City, New York 10001
(212) 655-5470 office • (516) 908-4496 fax
www.MorganJamesPublishing.com

Cover Design by:
Rachel Lopez
www.r2cdesign.com

Interior Design by:
Bonnie Bushman
bonnie@caboodlegraphics.com

In an effort to support local communities, raise awareness and funds, Morgan James Publishing donates a percentage of all book sales for the life of each book to Habitat for Humanity Peninsula and Greater Williamsburg.

Get involved today, visit
www.MorganJamesBuilds.com.

TABLE OF CONTENTS

Acknowledgements		*vii*
1	Why Can't We Be Friends?	1
2	An Enlightened Rescue Mutt	17
3	Having a Doggone Good Time	27
4	When the Lion Lies Down with the Lamb	39
5	What a Real Family "Feels Like"	47
6	I Love You, Deer One	57
7	How to Enjoy a Bear Hug	67
8	The Frog Prince Charming	75
9	How to Avoid Shell Shock	85
10	But We Are Only Human	93
About the Author		*111*
Giving Back – Ways for you to make a difference		*113*

ACKNOWLEDGMENTS

I thank all my furred, feathered, and scaled friends for the lessons that make up this book. I continue to learn from you each day.

I also want to acknowledge the humans who have been a part of making this book possible. I would not have begun the process without the initial support of Brendon Burchard, my publisher, who is also a gifted inspirational speaker, writer, and entrepreneur. Thank you, Brendon, for your continued support even after that first draft.

I am grateful to Michael J. Carr for editing this book. His love of words and animals, and his infinite patience, filled in the gaps left by an early childhood education that didn't thwart my creativity with fussy little rules on spelling and grammar. He is the best.

I acknowledge how lucky I am to have worked with David Hancock and everyone at Morgan James Publishing. I cannot even imagine a more supportive environment for an author.

I am eternally grateful to my wonderful family and friends for their support. To Brody—being your mom and watching you grow into such an extraordinary young man has been both a privilege and a pleasure. To my parents, my first teachers on how important animal family members are to us all. To Phil and Maria, who are wonderful in-laws, grandparents, and puppy parents. Without you and amazing women friends such as Terry, Charlene, Sheila, Caroline, and Anita, I could never have had many of the adventures in this book. You are the village that supported my two- and four-footed family members when I couldn't be there, and I am forever in your debt.

I am grateful that Michael Kobert, who is uniquely both animal expert and advocate, took time from his own passions to help me create this book. Michael you have a gift with animals and I am proud to call you family.

No words can express my appreciation for my sister Dona's hard work and support. While running your own business and doing your own conservation and television work, you still found time to search out the photographs that enliven the stories in this book. To me, they are the most special part of it, and I could never have done them without your help. Also, though I was skeptical at the time, I can now say without hesitation that I'm glad Mom and Dad brought you home instead of another puppy.

I am grateful for the relationship that didn't work out as I once thought I wanted. Our time together taught me valuable lessons, reflected in this book, and I will never regret having loved you.

To all the wonderful inspirational teachers whose books I have read and whose seminars I have attended, including Deepak Chopra, Marianne Williamson, and Gary Zukav, I am forever grateful. You helped me dig deep to find my truth, and sparked more life-changing thoughts than I can possibly credit you with. Please forgive me the many omissions you are bound to find in this book.

First, last, and above all, I am grateful to my husband, Patrick, whom I adore. You have always embodied the at once human and animal lessons of honesty, loyalty, and unconditional love. I am blessed that such a handsome, smart, funny, caring man chooses to spend his life with me. You are the finest human I know, and I love you.

Chapter One

WHY CAN'T WE
BE FRIENDS?

*Sheena the Lion Cub and Homer the Hyena
Pup Demonstrate Appreciation in Relationships.*

*I*t was a thrilling way to be awakened. He nudged aside the tent flap, letting in a beam of light that warmed my cheek and tickled my eyelids. I opened my eyes and saw him, backlit by the dazzling orange-gold of another breathtaking South African sunrise. He looked so handsome silhouetted there, batting those long, lush eyelashes! I slid out of my cot to greet him—and to keep him from laying his four hundred pounds of neck on me and licking me with that rough, eighteen-inch-long prehensile tongue. My morning visitor was, of course, my favorite even-toed ungulate: the majestic, one-of-a-kind giraffe. I walked outside my tent and stood on the attached elevated porch, which compensated some for the difference in our heights. From this vantage point, I shared some fruit with him and his mate. I also tossed food to the little stray dog that frequently showed up in the company of these two giraffes. While the pup was normally timid and skittish near humans, he must have felt safe enough with his adopted family, because he accepted my breakfast offerings. Even though he hid between hooves that could whip out with enough force to crush a lion's skull, the pup trusted its new giraffe "mom." I marveled yet again at how comfort and accommodation can be found in the unlikeliest places.

Shortly afterward, I started down the dirt road to the nursery of the lion sanctuary where I was working. I gravitated to Sheena, one of the ever-hungry lion cubs. I had planned to return to the United States as the hyenas' champion, because I felt they had gotten a bad rap in cartoon movies. And yet, I seldom selected Homer, the little hyena pup, to feed. I found it much more enjoyable to tend the orphaned lion cubs, with their soft fur and endearing *wha-ha* cry, than the hyena pup, with its wire-brush coat and demonic giggle.

I warmed a bottle of formula and cradled Sheena in my arms. Her paws rested alongside my hand as I lifted the bottle to her already sucking mouth. These early-morning feedings were magical times. Sheena finished her bottle, and I enjoyed the sweet scent of her warm breath as I raised her up to my shoulder to

stimulate a burp. As was her custom, Sheena snuggled in for a precious few moments before trying to add a new piercing to my ear.

The young woman who was taking care of the hyena pup that summer said she must leave, to attend to something urgent. Oh, and while she was away, would I mind monitoring the situation if she put Homer, the *hyena,* in the same enclosure with Sheena, the *lion*? My mind immediately wanted to dash off to all the reasons why I certainly did *not* want to be in charge of the welfare of two presumably instinctive enemies when they were placed together for the first time. *Remind me,* I said to myself. *How did I get into this situation?*

An Inner Jungle of "Dis-ease"

It all began six months earlier, when I booked my first trip to Africa. I could still hear the incredulous voice of Brody, my elementary-school-age son, yelling "Mo-o-o-om!" from the next room. You know you're in trouble when "Mom" all of a sudden has four vowels instead of one. My travel reservation had generated a fax from the U.S. State Department advising against travel to Africa. Brody walked into the living room, waving the fax and demanding that I explain why I was so intent on taking an obviously dangerous trip.

It was difficult to explain to a young child. Truth be told, I wasn't sure why I felt so ill at ease. I just knew that I was less afraid of venturing into the African wilds than of finding my way through the jungle of "dis-ease" that seemed to permeate my being.

I felt that over the past few years I had neglected, abandoned, and ultimately lost some of the most important relationships in my life. During that time, I had been a part of the caregiving team for a terminally ill young cousin. Cousin Ralphy was left weak and mostly hairless from intense chemotherapy to try to stop the cancer from spreading throughout his forty-four-years-young body. Somehow, though, he had kept those eyelashes that would make a supermodel jealous, and that sparkle in his eye. When he died, I felt overwhelmed by my inability to help him. I was also becoming afraid of how little impact I might have in creating a life with others I loved. My relationships had begun to make me feel as if I were journeying down a winding road with drunk drivers coming at me, leaving me feeling afraid and out of control. What if it turned out that I had lost the ability to create healthy, joyful relationships?

That sense of unease continued to grow, and I felt guilty about these feelings. After all, I had now settled back into my wonderful life, surrounded by a loving family. I had no right to feel this way. I comforted myself with the belief that I was handling my "dis-ease," and I was convinced that no one else had a clue about my inner struggles.

That is, until the day that our feline family member startled me out of staring blankly at the computer. Kitty had leaped up and knocked my computer mouse onto the floor. At first, I chalked this up to the fact that, being a cat, he had an innate disdain for anything known as a "mouse." But when, quite uncharacteristically, he stayed there on the desktop staring at me, I found it strangely disconcerting. Kitty eventually hopped down, only to return a few minutes later with the puppy in tow. Apparently, his "cat scan" had revealed that I was not all right and could benefit from a little puppy love. My dog, also sensing that one of its humans was not herself, put its wet nose in my lap and looked up at me with soulful, adoring puppy-dog eyes. It was clear that my furred, four-footed family members wanted me to recognize that it was high time to get to the bottom of these feelings.

In the past, I had traveled in search of life lessons, exploring how animals and indigenous people might live in harmony. I remembered how content I had felt on the beach at Acapulco, preparing my motivational talk on how animal companions illustrate for us how to put the "humane" back in humanity. Perhaps it was time to embark on another journey, this time for lessons on creating healthy relationships.

That's when I decided to travel to Africa for a few weeks, to observe wildlife in their natural environment, perhaps in Kenya's famed Masai Mara. My hope was to witness instinctive relationships based not on fear but on love and compassion. Perhaps I could heal my own sense of being ill at ease if I could find and focus on traits and attributes of a healthy world.

The flight to Kenya left a week later. I was atingle with excitement—right up until the first obstacle loomed up out of nowhere. As I was making the airline connection in London, the airline representative informed me that there were confirmed intelligence reports of a terrorist bombing planned that very night for an American hotel in Nairobi. Since an American hotel in Nairobi was where we would be spending the night, we might not wish to continue.

Okay, I thought, *here we go again.* While this was certainly disconcerting news, I was committed to my African healing adventure. However, it dawned on me that if I couldn't explain to my son why I should not let fear dictate my actions, I probably wouldn't be able to articulate my reasons to a stranger. So I found myself just blurting out, "*Hakuna matata,*" the way you might shrug and say, "I'm not concerned." The airline rep must have thought, due to my obvious knowledge of the native tongue, that I had made an appropriate risk assessment and decided to proceed. Fortunately, I wasn't obliged to confess that I had acquired my entire Swahili vocabulary from a cartoon warthog singing "No Worries" in a Disney movie.

After arriving in Nairobi for a blessedly uneventful night, I joined a group on a photo safari into the African bush. It was December, the dry season in Kenya. In the quiet isolation of the Kenyan plains, I realized I had found the perfect environment to begin my research on how indigenous African people and wildlife develop positive relationships.

One day we visited a group of Masai people. I learned that while it is true that a Masai man might take several wives, it is the first wife who picks the next—for very practical reasons. I met a Masai homemaker, in the truest sense of the word. She attempted to show how she had prepared the mixture of dirt and cattle dung used to finish the walls and roof of the house she had built. First, she mimed, we needed to loosen the dirt. She handed me a large, sharp pole to ram into the earth. I failed miserably. Apparently, years of Pilates exercises had not given me the arm strength of a Masai woman. She then took the pole from me and rammed it effortlessly into the hard ground until she had made a nice pile of loosened dirt. Afterward, she generously gave me a chance to redeem myself by mixing the loosened dirt with cattle dung, which lay all around us in abundant supply. I'm afraid my face must have reflected my reservations, because she walked away from me in disappointment. It was obvious: she wasn't picking me for her husband's next wife!

In time, this Masai woman would indeed select another woman to share both the obligations and the joys of life in her family. Though she spoke very little, she had unearthed for me an important truth: if we are unafraid to create harmonious relationships to support us in the challenges of life, then we, too, will have hit "pay dirt."

I decided to join the women of one of these blended families as they walked to the market, holding hands and laughing, with their children running about underfoot. At the marketplace, I fell in love with a pair of beautifully carved wooden giraffes. I was reluctant to ask the price, because I am an admittedly lousy shopper whenever negotiations are involved. But I was struck by the beauty of the pieces, so I asked how much. Sure enough, they were beyond my budget.

I thanked the craftsman who had made them, and started away. He rushed after me, demanding that I tell him what I wanted to spend. I explained that I was terrible at bargaining. "That is okay," he reassured me. "I will teach you." Not very comforted by the thought, I again tried to move on.

"Wait!" he demanded, "I will say one hundred, and then you say fifty."

Embarrassed, I obediently said I would pay fifty.

"Fifty!" he shouted, his voice filled with indignation. He explained what would happen to his small children if he accepted my insensitive suggestion of a price. Feeling terrible and also a bit confused, I started to back away, apologizing. The craftsman smiled and continued to instruct me. I realized that not only was I no longer interested in the carvings, I had become uncomfortable. I abandoned the idea of souvenir shopping, left the village, and spent the remaining week of that first trip enthralled by the amazing interactions of animals in the wild.

I witnessed fascinating behaviors, such as a zebra sounding a warning cry to a herd of migrating wildebeests, thereby foiling a leopard's attack. And I learned the amazing African love stories of Kamunyak the lioness and Naisimari the oryx, and Owen the hippo and Mzee the tortoise, which I will share in later chapters.

Eventually, the rain came, and the African bush was refreshed—as was my own sense of "ease." I boarded the airplane back to the United States with many examples of the "natural" love I had been seeking. I was convinced that I could continue to find among wildlife the manifestations of a healthy world that we all could incorporate into our own lives. I decided to return to Africa as soon as possible, to experience more natural situations in which love and compassion were the motivation for behavior.

A "Natural" Cure – the Instinct to Love

Six months after my return from that first trip, I found myself at the Lion Sanctuary in South Africa, working with orphaned and injured lions. That's how I ended up supervising as Homer, the hyena pup, was placed for the first time in the same enclosure with Sheena, the lion cub. Could a healthy relationship blossom under such unusual circumstances?

I tried to feel confident during Homer and Sheena's introduction. I waited to see whether these young "natural enemies" would respond aggressively to each other's differences, or find common ground. I didn't need to

wait long. Within seconds, hyena pup and lion cub were having great fun together. Sheena shared her toys even after Homer's playful bites on her ear. Homer initiated a game of tag, and they took turns chasing each other. Then I watched in amazement as pup and cub, with round, full bellies from their earlier bottle feeding, snuggled down together to sleep. I was so filled with love for homely little Homer, whom I had previously avoided, that I lifted him up and kissed his bristly hair, which now felt wonderful.

All three of us had been transformed by the experience. I was grateful to these two orphaned creatures for demonstrating how easily healthy relationships can come about when fear isn't a factor. Not having been taught that they were "natural enemies," hyena and lion became great friends.

At summer's end, I returned to the United States to share my experiences, giving motivational talks on how we can get along and form healthy, joyful relationships. I also began collecting other stories and lessons about unique animal friendships and families. Thanks to Homer and Sheena and so many other animals in Africa, I no longer felt "ill" at ease. I began to incorporate those animal lessons in my approach to the possibilities in my relationships.

You can go beyond supposed primal instincts of fear and mistrust and explore what happens when you substitute love and compassion. As you read the stories of my furry, scaled, and feathered friends in this book, you may come to experience a change in perspective that can help bring about your own healthy, joyful relationships.

Chapter Two

An Enlightened
Rescue Mutt

Lessons on Eliminating Self-Judgment

I have been on an ongoing quest to let go of my own self-judgment so I can better develop healthy relationships. I have learned meditation, become a certified yoga instructor, read books, attended seminars, followed my passion to work with wildlife, and set up a personal "table sanctuary." On that table, amid the flowers, written affirmations, candles, and pictures of loving family members and ancient spiritual teachers, is a photo of my favorite guru. He isn't exactly what one normally thinks of as a spiritual leader, although he certainly has a "Buddha belly." He is Benny, our rescue mutt. Unexpectedly, it was through his example that I learned one of the greatest lessons for eliminating ego: how to stop judging myself.

As a child, I had low self-esteem and viewed most events in my life through that imperfect lens. I tended to over think events and then judge myself harshly for coming up short. I would feel the sting for days if I wasn't picked first to be on a sports team. Hiding under the mask that I was a complete klutz, I let fear stop me from participating in athletics. I felt like the ugly duckling in my peer group. I had convinced myself that the only reason I had so many friends was because my best friend was so beautiful and popular. Being the sweet, funny, smart girl wasn't good enough—at least, not to my harshest critic: me.

This pattern of negative self-judgment followed me into adulthood, as such patterns are apt to do. Would the man I had wanted to share my life with have been able to commit to me if I had said something different, done something different, *been,* somehow, different? I wondered how many of my adult relationships were compromised because I wasn't lovable enough. Then I was lucky enough to meet Benny, a wonderful teacher of how to stop creating stories based on past fears and insecurities.

I know little of Benny's life before we met. His scars show that he had been badly abused. He was on "death row" at the pound before we adopted him. There certainly must have been a time when whatever Benny had lived through made him feel unlovable. His puppyhood had aged him prematurely and given him every reason to be sad, anxious, and distrustful. But rather than continue to identify with his history, Benny turned a corner. And now he's loving, patient, devoted, and joyful.

One windy winter day in Westport, Connecticut, my husband came home from work and announced that he wanted to take me to dinner. I hadn't planned on leaving the house that day, so I had skipped the whole hair, makeup, and clothes ritual and was still in sweatpants and an unflattering baseball cap when the invitation came. Patrick looked so handsome, I just didn't feel as though I looked nice enough to be his dinner date, so I declined.

Disappointed, Patrick suggested that perhaps we could at least take the dogs for a walk around the island. Hearing the exciting "w" word, Benny leaped up in eager anticipation, even though his wiry terrier coat looked rumpled and disheveled from his late-afternoon nap. Not the least bit concerned about his "bed hair" or worried that he wasn't living up to the image of dogs in "Pet House," he raced to the door. And during the walk, he didn't dash between houses or duck behind a hedge to avoid the perfectly groomed poodle heading our way. Benny enjoyed every moment of this unexpected treat that had landed in his lap, and his inner joy showed in the spring in his step and the wag of his tail.

When we returned from the walk, I bent down to wipe off each of Benny's paws. When he first came into our home he looked terrified during what must have seemed a bizarre, perhaps even dangerous, paw cleaning ritual. But now, with trust and love, he would lift each foot in turn to be cleaned. Exhausted, Benny (who has a pronounced underbite) allowed his thick tongue to hang out the side of his mouth. He looked so adorable, I found myself smiling. For a fleeting moment, I saw my own image reflected in one of Benny's big brown eyes. Though still clad in sweats and ball cap, I looked radiant, beautiful. So this was how my pup saw me! I looked over at Patrick, who was hanging up the leash on a hook in the mudroom. He smiled back at me, and I knew that it really didn't matter whether I was dressed in a sequined ball gown or running clothes—I looked beautiful to him, too.

"So, Patrick . . . ," I began. "About that dinner invitation . . ."

Patrick grabbed the keys in one hand, and my hand in the other, and laughing, we headed out to dinner.

Benny

Both Benny and my Samoyed pup, Briny, love these island walks. Last summer, I decided to walk them separately rather than endure their combined exuberance at the ends of their respective leases—which, more often than not, wound around me, making me look like some sort of animated Maypole.

Benny was the first to be left behind. He barked for a minute at the door to express his dismay and to alert me in case I had just somehow forgotten him. Although I don't know of any 12-step program he has attended, by the time I returned he was napping peacefully by the door, apparently having been granted the serenity to accept the things he could not change. Now he just looked up in anticipation, ready for his turn, and off we went out the door.

As we walked, I realized that Benny had apparently not wasted any time overthinking the situation. His ego didn't seem to be generating endless chatter that mired him down in harsh self-judgment. He hadn't beaten himself up wondering whether I had deliberately snubbed him because he was short and fat and had a questionable pedigree. He probably hadn't even wasted any time worrying whether I would rather be seen out and about with a more beautiful dog, like Briny. He wasn't jealous, nor did he judge my actions based on his past experience, wondering whether I had fallen out of love with him and was secretly planning to leave him forever. As far as I could see, Benny didn't appear to be letting the past diminish his enjoyment of the glorious, infinite present moment.

This was an important lesson for me. Now when I am afraid of moving beyond my comfort zone, I stop and think, *Is this just coming from my old habit of negative self-judgment?*

I've realized that the vision of me as the young klutz is only a memory—and an odd self-judgment, especially for a woman who has competed in triathlons and a marathon. The lessons I've learned from animals about self-judgment have helped me reenvision prior lost love as merely a result of circumstance, since I now know that I am worthy of commitment and deep love.

Don't let self-judgments formed from old experiences hold you back today. Past feelings of being unloved, being a "failure," or being a victim don't have to limit your current choices, emotions, and reality. Maybe, like me, you're even lucky enough to have your own domestic animal guru to look to for timeless wisdom on how to interact with your world. If not, I encourage you to adopt from one of the wonderful animal rescue organizations. The loving mixed breed, once scorned as a mere mutt, could easily be the designer dog of the future. More importantly, the new family member will bring life lessons through unconditional love.

Personally, whenever I need a reminder of how to release self-judgment, I just bend down, and Benny, in utter bliss, rolls onto his back for a "Buddha belly" rub.

Chapter Three

HAVING A DOGGONE GOOD TIME

*Briny the Smiling Samoyed and Kitty the Feral Feline
Demonstrate How to Live in the Moment*

I am a confirmed chocoholic, and I used to struggle mightily to abstain. It seemed the responsible thing to do. Part of me believed that I should wait until I had achieved my weight-reduction goal or accomplished some other important thing before rewarding myself with such indulgences. Another part wondered whether, had I been on the RMS *Titanic* as it sank, my last thought would be regret for declining the chocolate mousse the ship's stewards served earlier that night. This struggle usually ended with my liberating fudge or brownies stashed in veggie-burger boxes in the freezer, followed by a huge side helping of guilt.

I used to equate being responsible with postponing pleasure until I had finished whatever arbitrary tasks I had on my to-do list. Anyone who makes such lists knows that they are almost never finished—which, of course, meant that I frequently found myself missing out on pleasure in the moment. I often got frustrated with the pace of my progress and with the few paltry to-do items I had finished that day. Then, in an act of shameless self-appeasement, I would add something not previously on the list but recently done, just so I would have something to check off! This rarely worked. If I hadn't accomplished what I set out to do, I would punish myself by delaying gratification.

Thankfully, my domestic animal teachers have shown me how to live life in the moment. One such lesson came from an unexpected family member, Kitty, our cat with the Alexander Haig complex. I had always been more of a dog person and had never considered getting a cat. Then one day, when I arrived at the groomer's to pick up Justin, our big bear of a Samoyed, I found him happily playing with a little white ball of feline fur. Embarrassed, I tried to return the adolescent cat to the groomer. She informed me that Justin's newfound playmate was the abandoned kitten of a feral cat. Then she asked, since Justin liked him, could Justin keep him?

Not sure, I called my husband to get his opinion on whether Justin could have a cat. Distracted and on the other line with a business call, an incredulous Patrick

blurted out, "Justin wants a *cat*?" I assured him that apparently, Justin indeed wanted a cat, so we agreed to give it a try, but in case it didn't work, we would try not to get too invested in our newest adoptee. Thus, Kitty, with his rather unimaginative, noncommittal name, became part of our houseful of animal teachers.

Kitty and Justin were great friends throughout the last years of Justin's life, and when Justin passed away, Kitty was as devastated as the rest of the family. Deciding that perhaps a change of scenery would help, I arranged to take Kitty to a lake house we were renting in Connecticut. Now, taking a cat on a plane is more challenging than I realized. There were a lot of regulations to follow, paperwork to get in order, fees to pay, and a health certificate to acquire. We also needed to shop for an approved cat carrier. I worked diligently at the to-do list for moving Kitty and told myself that once we were there, I would treat myself to a midnight swim in the lake.

The morning of our departure, I tried to coax Kitty into his new carrier. I couldn't understand his reluctance. I had found a pet traveling bag that resembled a stylish sports bag, and I thought we would look pretty sharp. Kitty wasn't impressed. I cleaned up the floor where he had spit out the tranquilizing pills I had so cleverly disguised in tuna balls, and then managed to force Kitty into the carrier. As we set off on our airline adventure, I was feeling terrific. I had chosen an outfit that nicely hid the new scratches and Band-Aids on my arms, and it even went with the sports bag / cat carrier. Kitty was nervous. This was evident not just from his soft cries but from the strange warm sensation creeping down my leg, which seemed to come from the attractive—though, obviously, not waterproof—cat carrier. A stop at the restroom confirmed what anyone who has lived with cats already knows: no amount of soap and water applied with a paper towel will eliminate that smell.

As I rushed to the gate, I cocked my head toward the bag in an attempt to calm Kitty and repeated over and over, "It'll be all right . . . It's going to be all right." Since I was the only one who knew that my bag contained a live animal, I must have been quite the sight as I ran through the terminal talking to my shoulder. With this and also the smell, it was little wonder that the other passengers gave me such a wide berth.

When Kitty and I finally made it to the East Coast, I think we were both exhausted. It was dark when we arrived at the house, and the moment I liberated Kitty from his carrier, he promptly ran under the washing machine. Terrified that I had traumatized him and unable to get him out from under the washer, I knew better than to reward myself for such a lackluster performance. Defeated, I went up to bed.

Within minutes, Kitty sprang up the steps and curled up beside us, thrilled to have a bed with a view of night birds. As if the joy of his newfound panoramic Kitty entertainment center weren't enough, he looked up in rapture toward the rustlings coming from outside the back door. Eyes wide, he looked at me as if to say, "This place has mice, too? You thought of *everything*!" With an eager meow, he bounded back down the stairs and found a spot where he could sit in wait just in case a mouse should decide to pay a visit.

So, was Kitty still dwelling on his chaotic, stressful day? Not a chance! That was in the past, and he still had right now to enjoy these new and unexpected pleasures. I smiled as I went out the door where he had set up watch, and made my way down to the lake for that moonlight swim.

Briny

Briny, our new Samoyed pup, is our current master teacher of living in the moment. Described by some as a "holiday dog," a Samoyed has snow-white fur and a mouth that stays open in a sort of perpetual smile. Briny appears to be eternally happy and seems to love everything around her. This is so infectious that even our wild Kitty, who allows only select family members to come near him, will tolerate a thorough ear licking from Briny. I'm sure it is Briny's loving, joyful energy that encourages the harmonious cohabitation of all the members of our strange animal family.

Briny is a constant reminder of how not to postpone pleasure for some future time when I will deserve it more. I don't remember ever offering Briny a canine cookie and having her do anything but jump for joy. She doesn't

sit back in quiet contemplation, weighing whether she is worthy of such a treat. She doesn't deny herself the pleasure until she has taken off a few of those doggie pounds, nor does she punish herself for barking when I'm on a business phone call. For Briny, the past is past, and there is no point in postponing enjoyment for a future that may never arrive.

With Kitty and Briny's stellar example before me, I now try to embrace opportunities as well-deserved treats. While I still would be considered more austere than hedonistic, my new motto when it comes to enjoying the moment is that "excess is not nearly enough." I make fewer lists and take more moonlight swims.

So . . . are you waiting until the "right" time to enjoy life's special moments? Don't put them off. Your children will grow up, and you will miss time with them more than you will care about how clean your house was during those child-rearing years. And those impromptu brunches with friends and family you missed because of some business you had to catch up on? They are gone, and no amount of professional success will ever bring them back. And by the time you have finally knocked off all the things on your to-do list, your pet—or maybe *you*—may no longer be physically able to go for that run on the beach.

There's an oft-quoted adage that our pets live their lives by: "The past is gone and the future is unknown; all we have is now, and since it's a gift, we call it 'the present.'" When you find yourself about to put off pleasure, remember the lessons of our domestic friends and family. They know how to enjoy the moment—this one, right now. I think about that sometimes as I take a moment to nibble on a hunk of dark chocolate. Then I sit back and watch in amazement as Briny gives a good ear cleaning to her feral feline brother, whose trial period is now well into its tenth year.

Chapter Four

WHEN THE LION LIES DOWN WITH THE LAMB

*Kamunyak the Lioness and Naisimari
the Oryx Demonstrate a Parent-Child
Relationship Free of Expectation*

Photo Credit: Daniela Bateleur

I can still remember my toddler's soulful delivery of "Mama!" as he wrapped his little fist around my index finger and led me a few yards down the beach. He was excited to show me the seashells he had placed in a neat pile on the sand. We lay down on our bellies, and I asked him questions about the numbers, colors, and shapes in his collection. With his hair blowing in his face, and his cheeks pink from the sun and the excitement, he was clearly the most perfect child in the world.

Now, please don't misunderstand me. I still believe that my son is the brightest, funniest, handsomest child ever born. However, now that he is a teenager, I sometimes wonder if it was a mistake teaching him how to talk—and, worse, think for himself—especially if he is going to use those skills to compose legitimate-sounding arguments advocating choices that I feel are misguided.

As a parent, I know that boundaries are important to my child's growth and safety. I work hard at differentiating between what he needs and what I want for him. These latter lessons cannot be taught. They must be learned through personal experience. Showing him a picture of me as a teenager who believed that white lipstick was a legitimate fashion statement did not cue him that he might someday regret the pants-below-the-underwear sag as an outfit choice. So I decided to look to the animal world for examples of healthy parent-child relationships.

Kamunyak and Naisimari

I was in Kenya's Samburu National Park when I learned that a lioness named Kamunyak—in the local Samburu tongue, "the blessed one," had adopted a baby oryx named Naisimari. An oryx is an antelope, and legitimate prey for the king of the African savannah. Kamunyak, however, was utterly devoted to Naisimari, whom she treated as her own "cub." In the afternoons, the lioness would lie down for a nap, and Naisimari would curl up against her belly. Kamunyak was fiercely protective of her little one. She even went without food so she could defend her baby from other predators, including a leopard. Unfortunately, Kamunyak was weakened by weeks of looking after her baby, and wandered into a male lion's territory. How confused the male lion must have felt watching the lioness nurturing and entertaining her adopted young! You can almost imagine him roaring, "Don't you know better than to play with your food!" This first adoption came to a sad conclusion when the male lion killed the baby oryx. Kamunyak, in apparent anguish, came and sniffed the spot where the calf was killed, In time, Kamunyak would adopt other oryx calves to nurture with her maternal love.

Kamunyak must have sensed that the oryx would never become much of a hunter, as is expected of all young lions. But the love that the lioness had for her "children" was not based on expectations.

I love and am proud of my son. He will be successful on whatever path he chooses. For now, we have compromised, and as long as I don't see the underwear above the waistband, he can explore his own fashion sensibilities. With Kamunyak's example, I realize that while it would be negligent not to establish some boundaries for appropriate behavior; I cannot dictate my child's character or style of dress.

It is a challenge for us humans not to become disappointed by the unrealized (and often unrealistic) expectations we impose on our children. You might find yourself worried and angry at their choices and believe that it's because you just "want the best for them." But what your child longs for is to be accepted for who she or he is.

It is the happy ending of many books, movies, and true-life family dramas when the parent not only allows but celebrates the child's uniqueness. It is the working-class father in the movie *Billy Elliot*, weeping tears of joy as he recognizes his son's artistic talents. It is the beautiful book by the mother of an autistic child, describing her journey to a place she had not planned on visiting but which, she now recognizes, is the only place that could bring her so much joy.

One of my favorite images is the look of love that Kamunyak exhibits as the young oryx runs to her lioness "mother." Maya Angelou once shared with Oprah the importance of acknowledging your child with joy whenever they enter the room. Anyone who has ever had a dog has experienced that life lesson. A dog's feeling of happy exuberance when you return, whether it is from an extended trip or just taking out the garbage, is a wonderful example of unconditional love.

When your child enters the doorway, you need to let go of your expectations. Unconditional love is easy when you feel that sense of wonder at how your sons' and daughters' choices have defied the odds and led them home without letting them be eaten alive in the jungle of their lives. Your children's sense of self-worth is boosted when they realize you are happy to see them—not because of what you expect them to be but because of who they already are. An attribute of a healthy parent-child relationship is the ability to let go of expectation and celebrate your children without regard to whether they are cubs or calves.

Chapter Five

What a Real Family "Feels Like"

*How Mademoiselle Giselle the Papillon and
Finnegan the Squirrel Allowed Things to "Just
Happen" as a Symptom of a Healthy Family*

Dean Rutz / *Seattle Times*

*I*n high school, my son was on a very competitive swim team. That commitment involved my driving him to school in the predawn for a 5:15 practice. One morning, wanting to take advantage of our limited time together—and much to my son's dismay—I decided to converse. "How was your day yesterday?" I asked. His response was monosyllabic.

As we passed the park my headlights briefly illuminated a banner announcing a "Family Fun Picnic." *Okay,* I thought, *maybe I'll try an open-ended philosophical question.* "Honey, what do you think makes a family?" In the light of the dashboard, I saw the quizzical rise of an eyebrow before his head retreated even deeper into the hood of his sweatshirt.

I decided not to push the parent-child bonding, and the rest of the drive passed in silence. When we arrived and after he had hefted his two heavy backpacks out of the trunk, my son leaned his head into the window and said, "Parents and children who love each other." We both smiled.

My son had said much without having to elaborate on what makes a family. I remember, at his age, having my own very narrow definition—at least, of the family I planned to have. My future would include, after establishing my own brilliant career, marrying a handsome, successful man a few years older than I. We would have two children: a

49

boy and then a girl, spaced eighteen months apart. Each pregnancy would end in a natural childbirth, during the miracle of which I would undoubtedly hear angels singing the Hallelujah Chorus. We would have perfectly behaved pets. The entire family would do everything together, from vacations to volunteering for animal causes. My husband and I would celebrate our fiftieth anniversary in our home on the beach, where we would have lived those fifty years paying off the mortgage and planting each of our fifty holiday trees.

Well . . . , things didn't exactly go as planned. This morning, I woke up to the sound of a barge on the Huangpu River outside the window of the Shanghai apartment where I will be living for the next year. I rolled out of bed and woke my son—time to get ready for his holiday trip building houses with Habitat for Humanity in the Philippines. Stuffing a paper towel with the Chinese equivalent of Cat Chow, I took the elevator downstairs to feed my newest unexpected pet, a wild feral cat. Watching Chairman Meow, as I named him, eagerly accept his breakfast, I reflected on how children, animals, and love had come into my life not as I would have decided but as wonderful surprises.

Mademoiselle Giselle and Finnegan

Over the years, I have learned that if we just let it happen naturally, perfect families form themselves. One of my favorite animal illustrations of this began one September day in 2005 in Seattle, when a small squirrel was found, injured and malnourished. Finnegan the squirrel, as he became known, was lucky enough to be taken to Debby Cantlon, an area resident with a reputation for helping injured and orphaned animals.

Mademoiselle Giselle, Ms. Cantlon's pregnant papillon dog, became an unlikely nurse's aide. She would drag Finnegan's cage through the dining room, kitchen, and hallway to set it beside her own bed. Though Ms. Cantlon had some concerns about what might happen, she finally opened the cage. Mademoiselle Giselle was thrilled and adopted the baby squirrel as her "pup." Several days after the birth of her own litter, the new mother was seen encouraging Finnegan to nurse with her other babies. After they had fed, the squirrel and the five puppies would nap together. Finnegan didn't question his place in the family as he snuggled contentedly with his "siblings."

Our society's conception of family has changed and is still evolving. But if we allow family to be a function of love, it is as natural as a papillon with a litter that happens to include a baby squirrel. In the animal world, there are many examples of orphans being accepted by families of other species. These new mothers are known to nurse, protect, and play with the "different" baby with the same care they bestow on those they have given birth to. They illustrate how being a wonderful parent is about love in action.

How many people whose biological parents were not up to the task realize that it was really the grandfather, the grade-school teacher, or a friend's parents who raised them? It was not their biological relationship to the person but the person's love that taught them about acceptance and self-esteem.

One of my favorite examples is of a mom who, though she didn't give birth to her child, couldn't have loved him any more. The toddler, recognizing her as his primary caregiver, sensed that she would always be there to mother him. One afternoon, he came home visibly shaken after a visit to his biological mother's house. Gathering the small crying child into her arms, the "mom" tried to comfort him and sort out what had happened that upset him so. The little guy finally raised his eyes and, looking at her as if she were an illusion, reached out a finger to touch her face. With a puzzled yet immensely relieved expression, he cried out, "You feel real!" It turned out that his biological mom had told him that the woman he called "Mom" was not his *real* mom. At two and a half and very concrete, the toddler's frame of reference for someone not "real" was the characters in books and videos, who were only imagined and thus couldn't be there to care for or love him. But when he reached out to feel whether this mom was "real," his little finger and his heart confirmed that she was.

My son has grown up in an environment where "different" family groups were not all that unusual. He has known children whose parents were single, of different races or faiths, or of the same sex. In these families, as with Mademoiselle Giselle and her puppies, siblings did not view their situation as odd or unnatural. They took their example from the parents' acceptance. Children have to be taught that their family is different and therefore not "as good" as the traditional nuclear family. When that happens, the nontraditional child's sense of self-worth takes a hit. Most people and animals desperately long for love and acceptance no matter what their "family" looks like.

It's important to recognize that your family—or anyone else's—need not be traditional to be sacred. We should celebrate any opportunity to create a family of adults, children, and pets to share our lives. When you do not force families to look a certain way, but allow them to happen naturally as a function of love, you foster and nourish an important symptom of a healthy family.

Chapter Six

I Love You, Deer One

Tarra the Elephant and Bella the Dog
Show How to Let Others Complement
Your Life rather than Complete It

Used with permission/copyright The Elephant Sanctuary in Tennessee (www.elephants.com)

*L*oving someone is always, without exception, wonderful. Loving someone has never brought me a moment of pain. This is true even when I have chosen to be in a relationship with someone who did not return my affections or was deceitful, even abusive. "What!" you might ask. "Isn't that the very definition of the heartbreak of love? No, loving only brings a sense of warmth and joy. It is *dependency* on another to make us feel complete that brings pain.

In my twenties, I was too insecure to expose my complete self in a relationship. So I rationalized that I was showing deep love for someone by being empathetic to what they wanted in a woman, and then shoehorning myself into that mold, that image. This wasn't a total misrepresentation, since the aspects they needed were parts of me—just not all of me. When I began to feel incomplete, I would end the relationship. Ultimately, I realized that I had been cheating both of us by not giving the total me.

Not showing up as your authentic self can be the easiest thing when you are feeling incomplete and therefore "not good enough." Eckhart Tolle shares, in *A New Earth,* that our ego thrives on the attention of others. Rather than realize that the source of all energy is the love that is the true you, the ego seeks to have these needs met through role playing. But how fulfilling can a relationship ultimately be if we must resort to playing roles such as the villain, victim, or lover?

Through so many "animal lessons," I have learned that the most fulfilling relationships blossom between partners who are completely themselves and, therefore, not dependent on the other to make them feel whole. For example, Tarra's story is a beautiful example of how love without dependency can have extraordinary results.

Tarra and Bella

Tarra had been waiting outside under the balcony every day for three weeks. Her best friend was in trouble, and she wanted to be close. It is not unusual for elephants in captivity, as in the wild, to create lifelong friendships. At the Elephant Sanctuary in Hohenwald, Tennessee, elephants are often seen roaming in pairs. In this case, the situation was a little different. Tarra the 8,700-pound elephant's best friend was Bella, a Lab-mix stray.

The dog and the pachyderm were seen eating, sleeping, and playing together for many years. Unfortunately, one day Bella was found to have suffered a spinal cord injury. This meant that Tarra had to be separated from Bella, who was brought into the sanctuary's offices while she recovered. Bella's entire hindquarters, including her legs and tail, were immobilized, leaving her unable to walk or stand.

As the dog lay motionless, the founders decided to take Bella to see Tarra, who had maintained a constant vigil for weeks. The little dog needed to be carried and was laid down near her friend. Tarra lovingly stroked the injured pup with her trunk and gently tried to rub her tummy with a huge front foot. "I am here," the elephant seemed to be saying. "It doesn't matter if you can run and play with me; I love you as you are." Bella was so happy to be with her best friend that, to everyone's astonishment, she spontaneously wagged her tail.

Bella fully recovered, and she and Tarra were once again inseparable. Bella knew that Tarra loved her no matter what and asked nothing of her but her friendship. And for Bella's part, I'm fairly certain that her love for Tarra has nothing to do with the fact that hanging out with a pachyderm makes her pudgy puppy body look slimmer.

Tarra and Bella's relationship illustrates how, when people love without dependency, they can best support each other's healing and growth. It's a true fairy tale with animal characters.

Belle the Beauty (my favorite Disney fairy-tale heroine) enjoyed books and longed for personal adventure even when pursued by the most eligible village stud. She had no idea that if she fell in love with the Beast who loved her, he would be transformed into a prince. Love is a powerful agent in promoting change, but only if we don't expect or depend on a specific outcome.

Relationships with animals can help us humans realize how rewarding it is to show up as our authentic self. Many of us find this true not only with our domestic animal friends but also in our experiences with wildlife.

I lived for a year in a house in a wooded area, where a wild doe visited me daily. I called her Goldie Fawn, and we would share an apple. I didn't *need* these visits, yet each time, I recognized that they were magical. I didn't realize until years later just how much Goldie Fawn's beautiful, calming presence in my daily life had helped me through a turbulent year.

I wish everyone could experience how rewarding it is to have a "deer" friend. Their loving presence is probably why there are so many wonderful stories of deer and creatures of other species befriending each other.

Jasmine

One of my favorite accounts involved a greyhound found by police in Warwickshire, England. She was abandoned, malnourished, and trembling in a locked shed. The police took the traumatized dog to Geoff Grewcock, who ran the wildlife sanctuary nearby. Geoff and his staff took the dog in and named her Jasmine. Although she had suffered severe abuse, they were able to nurse her back to health. And once healthy and whole, Jasmine began to greet all new animal arrivals to the sanctuary with her loving presence. She would give a welcoming lick and, frequently, carry the new residents up onto the settee, where she would cuddle them. She even allowed newly arrived birds to perch on her snout. At this writing, Jasmine has already befriended five fox kits, four badger cubs, fifteen chicks, eight guinea pigs, two stray puppies, and fifteen rabbits.

Photo Credit: Peter Corns

I was not surprised to learn that her closest companion became an eleven-week-old fawn found semiconscious in a field. "They're inseparable," says Grewcock. "Brambie walks between her legs, and they keep kissing each other." Ultimately, when she is able, Brambie will return to life in the woods. Jasmine, meanwhile, will continue to extend her friendship to other new arrivals. Jasmine's love without dependence allows the new arrivals to release their fears and stress so they may begin to heal.

Animals are not afraid to be who they really are. In fact, they're incapable of being anything less. Their lessons show that true, lasting joy in a relationship is possible only when you show up as your authentic self.

You can't make someone else into someone you think you need. Nor can you be truly happy showing up for a person only in the way you believe they need you to be.

Don't be afraid to let another see who you really are. Try to see yourself as your companion animal sees you. You aren't fearful that you will reveal something to your pets that will jeopardize their love for you. The love of your animal companions certainly doesn't depend on your bank account, hairline, or body fat content. Try to release the ego and let your complete self extend to others. There is great joy in experiencing with people, as you do with your animal friends, a love that is unconditional.

Chapter Seven

HOW TO ENJOY
A BEAR HUG

*A Polar Bear and a Sled Dog, Letting Go of
Expectations Based on Experiences, Embody
Attributes of Healthy Relationships*

Photo Credit: Wayne R. Bilenduke/ Photographer's Choice/Getty Images

I have never enjoyed the dating scene. Even when I was officially single, I could best be described as a serial monogamist. In most cases, I was fortunate to experience joyful relationships. Even with the man who broke my heart, I was ready to "get right back on the horse" (or jackass, as my friends referred to him) once he came to his senses and wanted to try again. I never wanted fears based on my experience to prevent me from spontaneously enjoying the possibility of a healthy romantic relationship.

I have a friend who is convinced that all future relationships will end in the same heartbreak as her last one. She is never open to the possibility of a different outcome. I've seen her in action at a party. She meets a guy, and they begin the dance of exploration through conversation. Within minutes, my friend has stopped following her new acquaintance's words, because her mind has left the present moment and is well on its way down an all-too-familiar path. She imagines that this man finds her as stimulating as she finds him, and that he will ask for her phone number. She envisions their first date, how they fall passionately in love, have a tropical destination wedding, and buy a house together. Though she continues to look across the couch at his smiling eyes, she becomes suspicious as she imagines their mortgage, a puppy, a family. His moving mouth has become the symbol of future fights over inevitable issues involving money, time, or careers. Before they have finished that first drink, she imagines how they will ultimately endure a painful divorce and she will end up alone. When asked later if she likes the guy, she has long since decided: not well enough to have their yet unborn children spend every other weekend with him!

My friend preempts the possibility of pain and loneliness by refusing to take a chance that this person might somehow be different. By writing the story of how the relationship will end, she has manifested precisely the situation of loneliness that she most fears. It's hard for her to take a chance, but by never acting spontaneously, she can't be open to the possibility of a new and wonderful romance.

Polar Bear and Husky

A photographer in the wilds of Canada's Hudson Bay witnessed an unusual and unforgettable encounter on the frozen tundra that is one of my favorite animal lessons on acting spontaneously. Sled dogs were resting when a massive moving mound of snow suddenly came toward them. Then the terrifying reality hit: this was an adult male polar bear that probably had not eaten for quite some time. A husky moved in the direction of this threatening creature. The photographer lifted his camera to record what he must have feared could be a quick end to the dog's life. But what he captured on film appeared more like a play date between friends. The husky and the polar bear enjoyed a friendly romp, nuzzling each other and gamboling about in the snow. The polar bear must have enjoyed their little frolic, because he returned each night that week to play, continuing their joyful relationship.

If the husky in the Canadian wilds had decided from experience that he had reason to be terrified, he would have approached the polar bear with anger springing from that fear. But he didn't do as so many of us do, and begin to create a story line around the end of an encounter he had yet to experience: *Oh, sure, you act as if you want to be my friend. You think I'm going to believe you and get drawn into a relationship. But I know that no matter what fun and loving energy you're putting out right now, if I let myself be open to a relationship, you will ultimately be like all the other big, bad bears!*

The dog could have decided that by approaching in a vulnerable attitude he would be putting himself in danger and that, ultimately, the bear would attack. Thus, to protect himself, he might have approached the polar bear in a threatening attitude. His bared teeth and low-hanging tail would have signaled to the polar bear that he was preparing for a fight. The bear would have responded to the dog's hostile, threatening behavior with his own formidable teeth and claws, rising on his hunches and roaring, and diving into the fatal attack the dog feared. But the dog had not created this story line around an aggressive encounter he had yet to experience. Open and vulnerable, he had approached the polar bear with positive energy for this present experience. What resulted was an encounter that brought both animals joy.

Even though experience makes it difficult, we must remember that we are perfect just the way we are. The love that is our true self can be nothing less than perfect. When we let ourselves really *know* this truth, we give ourselves the freedom to act spontaneously. As author and self-help teacher Debbie Ford writes, when we allow even the most vulnerable parts of ourselves to show up, and open ourselves up to the belief that something wonderful might happen, the magic begins. We spontaneously create relationships based on *present* experiences.

Don't let yourself sabotage a possible joyful "bear hug." Be open to the most unlikely encounters. Be wise, but permit yourself to be vulnerable, Let go of the past, and be open to creating a new and wonderful romance—a true symptom of a healthy, joyful relationship.

Chapter Eight

THE FROG PRINCE CHARMING

*The Mouse and the Frog in an Indian Monsoon
Illustrate Loss of Interest in Judging Others*

Photo Credit: REUTERS/Pawan Kuma

everal years ago, we spent Thanksgiving at our Florida condo overlooking the Atlantic Ocean. One beautiful afternoon, I wondered where my son was and whether he might join me for a run on the beach. I knew from experience that Brody would respond more quickly if I texted rather than called. So, using my older-model cell phone, I typed "WHERE R U?" When he returned my call, I asked whether he was glad I had recently been making such a valiant effort to communicate via his favorite medium. "Good job, Mom," he replied. "Now we just have to teach you how to use the lowercase keys. I know you don't mean it, but when a message comes by in all caps I feel like you're yelling at me."

Being misunderstood is one of the dangers of what I refer to as "talking in thumbs." How differently we communicate now, not only within our families but in our businesses, too. There was a time when most business was conducted with people from similar communities sitting across the table from each other, able to hear tonal inflection and read body language. Today our business communities are global and our languages frequently different, and cultural differences can result in our making erroneous judgments about others.

I looked out the window again and realized we might have to postpone our run, since the winds over the ocean had begun to whirl, presaging a possible storm.

Then I smiled as I remembered a story reported by the AP wire service in July 2006. It's one of my favorite animal lessons on why it's good not to judge others.

The Mouse and The Frog

It took place during a sweltering India summer. During that time of year, it's as if the whole of India were lying still, able to keep only one eye open—an anxious collective eye, watching in anticipation. The hot air began to rise into the sky, colliding with the nearby ocean's cooler air. Then the skies darkened with clouds, and the torrential monsoon rains arrived. These rains are the life—and, sometimes, death—of India. Without them, there would be no harvest, which could mean millions dying of hunger. And yet, the rains can also wash away whole villages that lie in the path of mudslides and floods.

In the northern Indian city of Lucknow, people waited for the rains. The year before, a thousand had been reported killed by the monsoon in Mumbai. Already in 2006, over thirty deaths were reported. The rain fell on Lucknow faster than the land could absorb or drain it, and the water rose to almost knee depth.

A small mouse became stranded by the rising waters. Weighing probably less than two ounces and with its light fur damp and darkened from the water, it might have spent its last few minutes scurrying helplessly as the hungry waters consumed its little life. But to the amazement of onlookers, there appeared the astounding sight of the mouse's little pink, pointed snout watching over the bulging eyes of an unexpected rescuer. The mouse had apparently suspended judgment of its strange new benefactor and embraced this altogether unforeseen relationship. A frog had allowed the mouse to climb unto its back and, using its own amphibian attributes of buoyancy and webbed feet, maneuvered them both across the muddy water to safety.

So how, when our communication happens through technological media, do we find our way, safely and without judgment, across the rough waters of business? Technology is a wonderful tool for connecting our world in a global community. Just like money, sex, or power, it is bad only when it is abused.

We need to use our laptops, smart phones, and e-tablets as tools for reflecting rather than reacting. When I asked Brody why he didn't seem upset about my text, he told me he had reread it as if it were in lowercase, and realized that I probably just missed him.

I know how difficult it is not to respond the instant you have an indication that someone is trying to reach you. We all feel that our time is limited, and we don't want to miss out on a potential opportunity. And there are certainly different degrees of technological attachment, from the merely inconsiderate person who takes a call while having lunch with you to the downright menace who simply must return a text message while driving a car.

If you don't stop what you are working on to respond to every incoming call, text, e-mail, or instant message, you may find that you don't rush to judge others and are more focused and successful, both at what you were doing *and* at responding to the new message.

One day in Kenya, my truck had stopped near a tree where a pair of lions were mating. Although the act is only a few seconds long, it can be repeated every twenty minutes for three to five days. As I sat there watching, a gazelle walked by, apparently unconcerned that it might be considered prey. And indeed, the mating lions were uninterested. Now, at the risk of trying to read too much "between the lions," I have to think the male's ability to focus on the task at hand may have contributed to his success—in this case, in continuing his genetic lineage.

If we take a moment to try to evaluate business messages without judging the sender, we might be able to come to a better understanding. It also gives us opportunities to explore the meaning of cultural differences *before* we respond. If you get a message that your proposal has been received and that when you arrive in China you will be given the head of a fish for dinner, well, it's a good idea to do a little research before you respond—otherwise, you might not realize what an honor this is in the Chinese culture.

Dance of the Dolphins

Back home in Florida, I went to the window counter where I had left my phone after texting Brody about the weather change. Just as I looked out the window, a group of dolphins came looping by.

Watching their elegant ballet as they passed, I was reminded of an experience I had swimming in the Galapagos Islands. I had separated myself a bit from the others, who were snorkeling farther ahead. Just then a group of fins appeared in the water to the swimmers' left and began going toward them in that slow but steady motion that anyone who has ever seen *Jaws* subconsciously associates with the ominous *da-dam-da-dam* chords.

Before I could call out, the swimmers noticed the fins and panicked at what they judged to be encroaching peril. For several moments, I watched helplessly as they screamed and thrashed about in the water, tossing masks and knocking into each other with their swim fins. Then the most extraordinary thing happened: the approaching fins momentarily disappeared into the water as the beautiful, sleek bodies of a charm of dolphins rolled from their bellies onto their sides.

Our group must not have been the first people they had pulled this prank on. The dolphins appeared to have anticipated our reaction and were now jumping gleefully through the water and making the wonderful sounds of the playful mammals they are. The much relieved snorkelers began to laugh with these marine pranksters whom they had misjudged so completely.

In the new, globalized economy, there are greater dangers of a rush to judgment in business. Misunderstandings can be exacerbated by differences in culture, economic climate, and even the use of technology. Use the tools at your disposal wisely to make informed decisions. If you can refrain from making a quick judgment or an offhand retort, you may find that the person who appears to be playing the business role equivalent of the ugly toad may actually be a Prince Charming.

Chapter Nine

HOW TO AVOID
SHELL SHOCK

*Owen the Hippo and Mzee the Tortoise
Demonstrate Increased Susceptibility to Love
as a Symptom of Healthy Global Relationships*

Photo Credit: Associated Press

*O*ne of my favorite parables involves a troubled young student asking his spiritual adviser for answers to his dilemma. He explains that he feels as if there were two dogs battling inside him. One dog wants to live a peaceful life of compassion and love. The other dog rails against injustice with fear and anger. The student is concerned and wonders which dog will win. "That's easy," says the teacher. "The one you feed."

I was honored a few years ago with an award from a United Nations affiliate organization. It was for an address I had written on how the emphasis of the peace movement must be to find a way to befriend nations by addressing global needs. I called the speech "Waging Peace."

Based in part on the ideas in Deepak Chopra's book *Peace Is the Way,* I spoke about ending the *idea of war.* Chopra admits, this will be difficult, because when we are afraid or very angry, "We reach for war, the way a chain-smoker reaches for a cigarette, muttering all the while that we have to quit."

But to quit the habit, we have to believe that violence is not just an instinctive part of our own basic animal nature. How do you feed the desire for a compassionate response in a world where there are so many differences between people and nations? Owen the hippo and Mzee the Aldabra tortoise illustrated for me how even an unimaginable relationship is completely possible.

Owen and Mzee

In the winter of 2006, rising waters from the devastating tsunami in Southeast Asia had crossed the Indian Ocean all the way to the coast of Kenya, separating Owen from his mother. Rangers managed to rescue the terrified baby hippo and release him into Haller Park, an animal sanctuary outside Mombasa. Owen stood alone and confused until he saw another large gray mound and, filled with relief and joy, ran to find familiar comfort. The mound, however, turned out to be Mzee, who, like most Aldabra tortoises, preferred to be alone. Needless to say, he was not happy about the friendly overtures of a two-hundred-pound baby hippo. But Owen was not to be frightened away. He appeared persistent in his belief that a friendship was possible and that their differences were not as significant as what they had in common. When the ranger checked on them the next morning, Owen and Mzee were curled up together sleeping. After a few days in the tortoise's company, the frightened hippo had learned to relax, eat, and "come out of his shell." Owen began to nuzzle playfully under his new friend's neck—a favorite spot on many tortoises. Mzee would seek out places to sleep where Owen could snuggle up and feel secure. They discovered mutual pleasures, such as enjoying a swim together. Each animal could easily have hurt the other, but instead they formed a peaceful bond of trust and compassion.

A Compassionate Response

Any animal species can exhibit great differences in behavior depending on whether its circumstances are those of fear or of compassion.

Gay Bradshaw describes how elephants whose herds have been decimated—especially orphans who have watched the death of their parents from poaching—exhibit violent, asocial behavior. On the level of neuroscience, we can now actually map the marred neuronal fields, snapped synaptic bridges, and crooked chemical streams that are present in the brains of elephants exhibiting abnormal behavior. In an article in the *New York Times,* Eve Abe, once a child in war-torn Uganda, shows the parallels between the plight of Uganda's orphaned boys and that of orphaned elephants.

My experience at the Elephant Sanctuary in South Africa showed a very different instinctive response in an environment of compassionate concern. One sunny afternoon, I was offering food to a resident elephant. The elephant not only accepted my offerings; she passed the love forward. She would alternate eating the food from my hand with placing offerings inside the mouth of a nearby elephant whose own truck could not function, because it had been severely damaged by a trap.

Animals illustrate that when kindness is present, there remains hope for interspecies and global relationships. Jane Goodall, a UN ambassador of peace, shares a story from her book *Reason for Hope*. She describes a lesson she learned from Greybeard, a chimpanzee in Tanzania. One day as they sat beside a stream, Jane picked up a nut off the ground and held it out to the chimp. Greybeard dropped it—only to take her hand instead. "He didn't want the nut," Goodall said in an address in Manhattan, "but he understood my motivation; he knew I meant well . . . We had communicated in a language far more ancient than words . . . a language bridging our two worlds. And I was deeply moved."

We can choose to focus not on our differences but on the fact that animals and people of every country, religion, and culture want to provide their families with food, shelter, drinkable water, safety, and a livable earth. When we emphasize addressing universal needs we open the door to living together in peace. Even our own sense of security will increase when we are recognized not as a threat but as a member of the global family.

In our eyes, a hippo and a tortoise lying on the grass create gray mounds that are very different. But Owen and Mzee chose not to be limited by their differences. By discovering what was important to each of them and finding ways to help meet each other's needs, they found their own joy and contentment.

Obviously, there are no easy solutions to finding global peace. Great effort and great resources are required for nations to be successful in any campaign, whether of violence or of compassion. Animal lessons, such as Owen's campaign to win over Mzee, illustrate how we must persist in the belief that friendship is possible and that our global differences are not as significant as what we have in common. We must place our emphasis on feeding the desire for compassion. When we befriend other nations, we open the door to creating healthy global relationships.

Chapter Ten

BUT WE ARE ONLY HUMAN

*Photographs of Unique Animal
Relationships Incite Overwhelming
Episodes of Smiling—
a Clear Symptom of Health*

Photo Credit: Dr. Ronald H. Cohn/Gorilla Foundation/koko.org

*M*ost days at the beach, I leave the house barefoot and then embarrass myself by leaping and hopping to the water's edge, trying to keep my feet off the hot sand. One particular morning, though, a cloud cover kept my feet comfortably cool. Since the cool air was causing my skin to rise in goose bumps, I decided not to enter the water yet. I spread my towel on the sand and sat down to think about the conclusion to this book.

I had planned to end the book with pictures of animal relationships that were sure to generate an overwhelming urge to smile. I loved all the pictures, but I still worried about finding the words to sum up this book. I had hoped that a swim would clear my head, but the swim would have to wait until the sun returned.

As I looked up to calculate when the sun would next peek through the clouds, I realized a simple truth: the sun wouldn't "come out again"—it was already there. It was always there. The clouds might obscure it, but it hadn't gone anywhere.

I began this journey feeling a sense of unease permeating my entire body. I now see that it was fear that had "clouded" my perceptions and created the sense of "dis-ease." Through animal lessons, I had learned that a healthier choice, like the sun, had always been there.

When I felt most lost, Sheena the lion cub and Homer the hyena pup had illustrated that it is not just part of our "animal nature" to react with fear. Healthy and joyful relationships can take root even in the unlikeliest places.

Witnessing instinctive relationships based not on fear but on love and compassion has changed how I view what is possible for me and for all humanity. I now believe that if we follow these examples from both wild and domestic animals, we can achieve *anything,* from inner harmony to global peace.

On a personal level, Benny, my enlightened rescue mutt, had shown me how not to limit myself through self-judgment formed from experiences of fear and insecurity. Just as his abused puppyhood didn't stop him from being the joyful, trusting dog he is today, we should not allow a tortured past to define us. Just like Benny, I was able to let go and create a new life of harmony.

My other domestic gurus continued to illustrate aspects of inner peace. Briny the Samoyed pup and Kitty the feral feline were constant reminders of how I could live in the moment. Just as Briny never questions her worth before accepting a treat, and just as Kitty would not let our stress-filled plane ride dampen his joy once we landed, I no longer have to clear a to-do list before rewarding myself. My pets' examples have reminded me that opportunities to enjoy this present moment will pass whether or not I take advantage of them.

My relationship with my family has grown closer thanks to the lesson of Kamunyak the lioness and Naisimari the oryx. They illustrated for me that by imposing expectations on my son I would devalue his life choices. Just as Kamunyak's love did not depend on Naisimari's performance or appearance, it is not my role to dictate my child's life journey. It's up to him to decide what will make him feel relevant and joyful.

Mademoiselle Giselle the papillon and Finnegan the squirrel continued to show what can happen when we celebrate even the most unconventional families. The unbridled joy that our dogs give us is never contingent on how we look or what we have accomplished. Similarly, I found that the unconditional love and acceptance that came when I let go of expectations only improved my healthy relationship with my child.

A more joyful bond in romance and friendship has resulted from incorporating lessons such as that of Tarra the elephant and Bella the dog. Their friendship shows how the role of a good relationship is not to *complete* but to *complement* each other's lives. Just as an elephant's tireless vigil caused an injured pup to wag her tail, love without dependency can be a powerful agent in creating a magical space that promotes my own relationships' growth and health.

By incorporating the experience of the polar bear and the sled dog into my adult relationships, I have also learned how important it is to let myself be vulnerable. By letting go of my experiences, I can spontaneously create relationships based on the present.

It takes much less effort just to stop protecting myself— and it is vastly more rewarding. By going through life with my metaphorical teeth bared in anger, or my tail held low in fear and mistrust, I was guaranteed to recreate negative experiences. I now try to live my human relationships with the same confidence I feel with my pets. Just as I don't fear revealing something that might jeopardize my dog's or cat's love for me, I know that showing up as my authentic self can only enhance my friendships and romance.

In my business dealings, I now remember the lesson of the mouse and the frog in the Indian monsoon and suspend judgment of others. I have found it much easier to navigate the strange waters of a global economy by allowing the possibility of new and unusual business partnerships.

And finally, through the examples of such wonderful friendships as Owen and Mzee's, I am convinced that it is possible to create a healthy global relationship by addressing each other's needs. The hippo and the tortoise found a way to go beyond their considerable differences and focus on their common concerns. When one species reaches out in compassion to address the needs of another, a bond of love and trust forms. If nations reach out to each other with compassionate diplomacy, similar bonds of friendship become possible globally. If we recognize how love can be a greater instinctive response than violence, we can create a successful global family.

Never lose sight of the peace and joy that are your true nature. Animal examples of compassion and love may seem easier for furry, feathered, or scaled friends than for us. You may have to work harder at these choices—after all, you're only human. Ultimately, when you change your perspective your own "animal nature" will respond, and you will instinctively recognize and create the symptoms of healthy, joyful relationships.

TEN SYMPTOMS OF HEALTHY, JOYFUL RELATIONSHIPS

1. Frequent, overwhelming episodes of appreciation
2. Loss of interest in judging yourself
3. Ability to enjoy each moment
4. Cessation of worry and disappointment stemming from unfair expectations
5. Increased tendency to *let* things happen rather than *make* them happen
6. Loss of dependency on another to complete rather than complement your life
7. Tendency to act spontaneously rather than from fears based on experiences
8. Loss of interest in judging others
9. Increased susceptibility to love given by others, and the uncontrollable urge to give love to others
10. Frequent overwhelming episodes of smiling

I hope you enjoy the photographs of these unique animal teachers of healthy relationships. I almost always find myself grinning from ear to ear. If I had a tail, I'm sure it would be wagging wildly.

101

Photo Credit: Dimas Adriane/Stringer/Getty Images News/Getty Images

Photo Credit: Photoshot

Photo Credit: Newspix Australia

Photo Credit: www.noahs-ark.org

Photo Credit: Phil Noble/Press Association Images

Photo Credit: Phil Noble/Press Association Images

Photo Credit: Anne Young/Solent News

About the Author

Denise Donato-McConnell has worked with numerous organizations dedicated to improving the lives of animals. While traveling the world in search of animal stories, she has worked with lions in Africa and published a series of articles including lessons learned from time spent with pandas in China. An award winning speaker and author, Denise enjoys bringing to her audiences the humor and insights gained from the natural world.

www.DeniseDonato.com
www.GigglingGorillaProductions.com

Australia

Africa

China

Bali

111

GIVING BACK

A percentage of all profits for this book is donated to organizations involved with animal rescue and rehabilitation. From the bottom of our hearts, we thank the following dedicated groups. We encourage you to visit their Web sites to discover more about their important work and to donate as generously as you can to their missions of love.

1. Humane Society of the United States
www.HumaneSociety.org

The nation's largest animal protection organization. It works to reduce suffering and improve the lives of all animals by advocating for better laws, investigating animal cruelty, conducting campaigns to reform industries, providing animal rescue and emergency response, and

caring for animals through sanctuaries, emergency shelters, wildlife rehabilitation centers, and clinics.

2. The Gorilla Foundation
www.Koko.org

Dedicated to the preservation, protection, and well-being of gorillas, its mission is to bring interspecies communication to the public in order to save gorillas from extinction, and to inspire our children to create a sustainable future for all great apes.

3. The Elephant Sanctuary, Hohenwald, Tennessee
www.elephants.com

The nation's largest natural habitat refuge developed specifically for endangered African and Asian elephants. The sanctuary provides a haven for old, sick, or needy elephants in a setting of green pastures, dense forests, spring-fed ponds, and heated barns. It provides education about the crisis facing these social, sensitive, passionately intense, playful, complex, exceedingly intelligent, and endangered creatures.

4. Nuneaton Warwickshire Wildlife Sanctuary
www.NuneatonWildlife.com

Committed to improving the lives of animals, whether by providing a safe and loving foster home or thoughtful relocation via adoption, adoption networking, and medical care. The people are passionate that all animals  experience humans as kind and loving friends. Run completely from donations, the sanctuary's goal is to expand its resources as a "no-kill" sanctuary and broaden its educational programs. They believe with conviction that no animal should be born simply to die.

5. Noah's Ark, Locust Grove, Georgia
www.Noahs-Ark.org

 Noah's Ark is an animal rehabilitation center and a partner for a children's care home. It provides a home for abused, unwanted, and orphaned animals. The folks there work to create an awareness through rehabilitation and education programs emphasizing that all living things, no matter how small, have value. They believe that if we, as a society, can recognize this fact, we will begin to win the battles for conservation and preservation.

6. Humane Society International
www.HSI.com

Humane Society International is one of the few international animal protection organizations in the world working to protect all animals, including animals in laboratories, farm animals, companion animals, and wildlife. Its record of achievement demonstrates its dedication and effectiveness.

7. Jane Goodall Institute
www.JaneGoodall.org

Founded by renowned primatologist Jane Goodall, the institute is a global nonprofit that empowers people to make a difference for all living things. It works to improve understanding and treatment of great apes. It contributes to the preservation of habitats through education and promotion of sustainable livelihoods in local communities, as well as through a worldwide network of young people who have learned to care deeply for their human community, for all animals, and for the environment.

8. The Lion Park, Johannesburg South Africa
www.Lion-Park.com

Goals of the Lion Park include increasing the understanding of African wildlife and educating the public on the conservation of ecosystems where such

wildlife resides. Lions, cheetahs, wild dogs, hyenas, giraffes, and indigenous antelope are given a natural environment. The park also has a breeding program for the white lion.

9. Wolf Mountain Sanctuary
www.wolfmountain.com

WMS is a non-profit 501©3 educational organization dedicated to the preservation and proper management of wolves in the wild and in captivity. The ultimate goal is to save these great, noble animals from extinction.

Photo Credit: Roger Tertocha

Printed in the USA
CPSIA information can be obtained
at www.ICGtesting.com
JSHW012013140824
68134JS00024B/2391